THE BUSINESS ALLOTMENT

TIPS FOR BUSINESS START UPS:
LESSONS FOR LIFE
BY
DR. NICK OWEN MBE

Introduction.

Starting a business is much like working an allotment. You have a seed of an idea; you nurture it in a little clay pot until it struggles into the daylight; you stress about providing it with enough manure in the form of funding so that you can eventually transplant it into the wicked, wider world of the adult vegetable patch with all its attendant predators, parasites and pitfalls.

With any luck your seed of an idea makes the journey from an innocuous looking bulb into a strapping gladioli which flowers annually with the minimum attention from you, allowing you to tend to other seeds or sit back and bask in the glory of your potato crop.

Often though, that process of business incubation is all too fraught and too many seeds of business ideas fall on the rough ground of customer disinterest or are devoured by the foxes of enterprises which are faster and more cunning than you when it comes to protecting the febrile business that is struggling into the daylight.

This book introduces various tips and tricks which are designed to help you start and protect that business of yours. It's an allotment because your business – anyone's business – cannot survive alone but needs other businesses of different shapes, types and flavours to flourish.

An allotment allows for cross trading, cross fertilisation, mutual collaboration and the sharing of ideas in ways which might sound misplaced in the context of a cut and thrust, capitalist market place: but one thing all entrepreneurs know deep down is that they can't do what they do alone.

They need the input of others, whether this be in the form of shoveling up the shite, digging protective trenches against the voracious slug or simply holding an umbrella over you as the sun burns down on your life long desires.

They need manure – obviously – but also need a collection of sharp and blunt tools, good quality soil, an absence of wasps nests and a good supply of that magical ingredient, water. So simple, so obvious and yet so mysterious – water is to the allotment what vision is to the business.

There's no guarantee these tips and tricks will work; but if at the very least you can see your business start up as your very own allotment – and not your own private back garden – there is every chance your business will make it through the winter and be around next summer for you to sit in and admire your burgeoning brassicas.

Of course, starting up your business is also very much like trying to steer your life, irrespective of whether you're in business or not. So, I hope this book helps you navigate your life as much as they are intended to help you tend your beautiful business idea.

Happy Allotmenteering!
Dr. Nick Owen,
Nottingham, UK

CHAPTER ONE: STARTING UP

Eight Tips and Tricks for Business Start Ups

1. *Reasons to (start up your) biz cheerful*
2. *Forget the clichés*
3. *If you wanna get ahead, get an algorithm*
4. *Don't flounder in the Founder Syndrome*
5. *Find your Inner Mountaineer*
6. *Life's a pitch and then you die*
7. *If in doubt say 'Creative'*
8. *How to love your Business Plan*

Reasons to (start up your) biz cheerful.

Why don't you get right out of bed?,
Why don't you get right out of bed? (x5)
Reasons to be Cheerful (Part 3)

Son of Richard Branson
Looking rather handsome
Never ending dreaming
Nottingham visioning,
driving up your missioning
Scribble out your plans

Partnerships sole traders
putting on your waders
Ignoring all the fakers
Blue chips on the rich list
Internet top lists
with your SEOs

Printing all your t shirts, stopping where it hurts
Dressing up in suits, office flirts
Dressing to impress, dining to invest
Investing your time, paying no fines

Designing handsome logos, customers going loco
dance an office pogo
Cash flow and income, spending all you've got
Fascinating knots, balancing the sheets

Reasons to biz Cheerful (Part 3) x 3
Reasons to be Cheerful – one, two, three

Reasons to biz Cheerful (Part 3)

Martha Lane fox, Changing your socks
Mending the locks, Calling the shots
A bit of grin and bear it a bit of come and share it
You're welcome, do come again, red reminders
Too small for VAT, PAYE
Going all legit, no nasty shocks

The never ending day, emails all the way,
Working in your car, driving afar
thrashing your laptop, Sit down take a break?
you're having a laugh!

Looking for investors, all other tasters
Splitting the difference, taking lots of punts,

spotting opportunities,
Facing up to dragons

Duncan Bannatyne, Hilary Devey,
Theo Paphitis, Deborah Meaden,
Peter Jones

Reasons to biz Cheerful (Part 3) x 3
Reasons to be Cheerful – one, two, three

(with immense thanks and respect to Ian Dury,
of course)

Forget the Clichés.

Carla slumped into the chair at the end of a miserable day and looked despondently into her mirror. Her unique make up offer (Stickless Lipstick) was looking distinctly unimpressive: sales had slumped, her website designer had started to resemble the Jurassic Park Fat Controller and her overseas supplier had clearly decided to up sticks and move to the Himalayas for all the communication skills he was demonstrating.

She wondered, not for the first time this week, this month or indeed this year, whether this new business start up business was all it was cracked up to be.

But this is all in a day's work for the aspiring entrepreneur. There will be many days when sales suck, profits revert to losses and your products look pathetic. There'll be days when the clichés fly thick and fast as you attempt to hold onto any motivational cliché you can summon up at two in the morning when the kids aren't sleeping, your partner's out boozing and the cash flow is freezing before your very eyes. *'Dream It Large'; 'No Sleep Till Christmas; 'Pull Out Your Hair Until Your Head Bleeds':* will all come flooding into your consciousness and add to your general feelings of inadequacy and defeat.

But this is all fine and should be welcomed by the aspiring entrepreneur because after all, you're allowed to have bad days: very bad days in fact. You're allowed to feel a failure and not step up to other people's plates and you're allowed to disappoint as many people as you can before breakfast.

Building your business is not about pleasing others but looking at yourself in that mirror and accepting yourself, warts, beauty spots and peculiar skin blemishes and all.

After a long days night of trawling around the internet, Carla subsequently found her own source of aspirational aphorisms to slow her to sleep and face the next day with renewed vigour and purpose in the form of Brian Eno's Oblique Strategies.

'Imagine a caterpillar moving' rekindled her internal locus of control; *'Repetition is a form of change'* was a comforting reassurance that even the biggest thinkers of the era aka Albert Einstein can sometimes get it disastrously wrong; *'Pay attention to distractions'* allowed her to stop obsessing with the orthodoxy that expects obsession: and *'Disconnect from Desire'* jolted her into remembering that having a desire for your business is one thing but that sometimes desire can get in the way of allowing things to happen of their own volition.

Carla's current fave track is Pharell's HAPPY is fantastically infectious and a great incitement to keep your spirits up: but sometimes its OK to realise that there are very good reasons to be miserable about the state of your business. It won't be the end of the world and it won't be the end of your business, or indeed your life.

If You Wanna Get Ahead, Get an Algorithm.

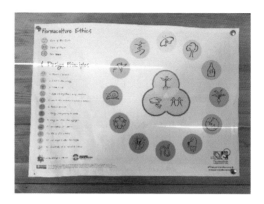

There was a time when all the fledgling start up business needed to start up was to set out their stall, woo their customers and count the shekels as they tumbled through the door, unencumbered by any thoughts at all about the internet, the world wide web and e-commerce.

There was a time when all the fledgling business start up worried about was how they could attract investors using the latest gee whizz bang words which would automatically guarantee them a place at the top table of the annual dinner dance of their local chamber of commerce. These gee whizz bang words used to be things like *'non-stick'; 'Made in Great Britain'* or *'as shown on TV'*.

Not any longer: the fledgling business these days has to concern themselves with matters much more ethereal and phenomenological. These days, if you want to get ahead as a fledgling business start up, you need to get an algorithm.

Chris is a case in point. Chris has recently set up a new business which makes remarkable claims: he has invented a little black box which, when plugged into people and the internet alleviates their hunger in a matter of days.

In one fell swoop, Chris has solved world hunger. And how has he done this? The little black box has nothing remarkable about it: a few flashing LEDs, a couple of discreetly placed on/off buttons, a power cable and a modern logo which doesn't tell you much about anything.

No, it's not the box that does the business: what Chris will confidently tell you is that its what's inside the little black box: its a combination of cheap Arduino sensors, valves, diodes all driven by a killer piece of software: the algorithm.

Chris claims that his software developers have developed some world beating software which has miraculously emerged as the World Hunger Algorithm: all from their laptops parked at a service station somewhere up the M6. This algorithm will, at the slightest encouragement dispel your hunger for days at a time whilst miraculously keeping you fit, healthy and sated.

Chris has tapped into the sources of modern day magic: the algorithm and is currently traveling the length and breadth of the country looking for investors to back his world beating, Nobel Peace Price winning, doubt inducing, bank account emptying little black box with his algorithm hidden somewhere inside it.

If you meet him in a pub one night, beware of his claims and whatever you do, don't allow yourself to be plugged into the internet in the belief that you're about to lose all those calories you've been pouring down your neck since you left work on the next round of Christmas parties.

Don't flounder in the Founder Syndrome.

That every business start up is started by someone, two or three people is a given on the Business Start Up Allotment. No business exists until such time that one bright spark will say *'let's do this and I want to do that'* and off they trot, firing on all cylinders as they dispense largesse, grace and favours to anyone who will listen to their persuasive rhetoric for more than a minute or two.

Before long their dream is up and running the streets, the website is out in cyberspace and the business cards printed with themselves named as Founder, CEO, Managing Director, President (sometimes all four) or whatever power handle takes their fancy.

The Founder Syndrome problems start at this early act of naming themselves. The titles of CEO or MD are roles in an organisation and can be passed onto someone else, once one CEO decides he or she has had enough and is put out to pasture. They're temporary names that can be as easily removed as gained and reflect the skill, expertise and relevance of the post holder.

The title of Founder though isn't a role: it's a statement of ownership and possession and no matter what happens in the future, the title cannot be taken away by any young buck who fancies the title. That young buck may well be successful in taking on the CEO role – but they'll never become the Founder.

The Founder is able to exert permanent claims to ownership from day one of the start up venture. This in itself is not necessarily a problem: benign founders are able to share their vision with others, are prepared to have that vision critically challenged and mature enough to be flexible in delivery whilst keeping steady on the long term strategy.

Benign founders are less concerned about the image of being a founder and more concerned about doing the right thing in the right kind of way.

Benign founders will invariably have a knowledge or skill base upon which they argue for and promote a vision for their business.

Benign Founders are not only persuasive and generous, but tend to be interesting and inspiring people to be around, given their views on and experience of the world.

Malign Founders however are a different kettle of fish altogether and worth steering clear of for a variety of reasons.

They see their vision as their personal property which will only be shared with people who are inclined to nod their heads more than shake them; the Malign Founder cannot be challenged in any way whatsoever and construes challenges as disrespecting their authority, not recognising that respect is earned through actions, not demanded through fear.

Malign Founders are driven 247 by what things look like and how they are perceived. For the Malign Founder, Image is Everything.

Malign Founders may, when you scratch their surface, have a negligible knowledge or skill base to operate from and before long will be issuing demands and diktats which are based on nothing other than what ever takes the founders fancy that morning.

Malign Founders consequently tend to end up as flounders: flat fish which wallow in the shallows and invariably get washed up on the Beach of Irrelevance, puffing in the sand, blowing hot air to any passing stranger who has a spare minute or two to listen to their woes of how it's everyone else's fault that the start up of the malign founder has collapsed under the weight of its own rhetoric.

So, be careful of those Founder Fish in your dealings with start ups: spotting the different between the Benign and the Malign variety will be essential if you don't want to be struck down by food poisoning for the rest of your start up venture.

Find Your Inner Mountaineer.

Goal setting is a tried and tested management technique which is a pretty useful device to help you clarify what you want to achieve in your business. The trick with goals though is that once set, you shouldn't look at them again until you've achieved them.

It's like mountaineering: if you keep looking up at the summit you're trying to conquer you'll throw yourself off balance and just topple over backwards and be destined to start the process all over again.

Bill is a case in point. He's set himself a target of 50,000 sales of his unique flower pots in the first year of trading. The target is ambitious and challenging: so much so that he's being stretched this way and that in trying to reach it.

He stresses and strains but that figure of 50,000 looms larger and larger day by day. It never shrinks but just stands there: implacable, ponderous, sneering, much like Mount Everest, daring to be overcome. And for the first month or two this implacable target drained away Bill's confidence, belief in the superiority of his flower pots and will to live.

He promoted and promoted, pushed and pulled and yet that damn target stood there, ridiculing him until one day, Ben phoned Bill and ordered a dozen for his new greenhouse.

The first sale took it's time to complete: but complete it he did and by the end of the week, Bill was 12 flower pot sales closer to his target. At this point he stopped thinking about the summit, but just concentrated on the next step: the next dozen flower pots to the neighbouring allotment.

That sale happened surprisingly quickly and before he knew it, Bill was taking one step at a time towards the summit of 50,000 sales: but the trick was to stop looking at that mocking target and just focus on the here and now of today rather then the promise of impossible riches tomorrow.

Before his first six months were through, Bill realised that 50,000 was way too pessimistic a target and that it needed revising upwards. So up went the target but this time, instead of fretting about the sheer impossibility of it all, Bill knew that all he needed to do to achieve his goals was to stop looking up at them, keep looking down at the ground beneath his feet and set off, one slow, laborious step at a time.

Life's a pitch and then you die.

There's no getting away from it, but if you're starting up a new business you'll be expected to pitch, pitch and pitch again to all sorts of people in all sorts of contexts for all sorts of reasons.

Until you have pitched your business proposal to your mother, her bright idea to your dad, and his eureka moment to your bank manager you will not be deemed to be a start up worth your salt.

Pitching has become the litmus test of the entrepreneur's intentions, ideally indicating a compelling economic future. Without the watertight pitch, the entrepreneur's aspirations just become the flotsam and jetsam of the flood plains of the Somerset Levels, washed up on the kitchen table or floating down the street collecting yapping dogs or stranded grannies along the way.

Pitching – the process of summarising a business proposition and ending in a big ask – can be useful in helping crystallise why you're doing what you're doing and communicating that rationale in as succinct fashion as possible.

But it's based on the premise that you have something valuable to say to people who are worthy of hearing it but who don't have the time or attention span to give it the time it deserves.

Your pitch has to deliver its promise unapologetically: and then get the hell back to Kansas as fast as it can because, after all, you're talking to very busy people who have much better things to be doing.

Pitching has become to business thinking what MacDonald's has become to haute cuisine: high carb and high fat delivering a sugar rush of big promises and inflated bank balances in the time it takes to travel from the tenth to the ground floor of your friendly neighbourhood economic regeneration agency. Pitches generate wind, hot air and impossible deals of undeliverables in equal measure.

If you measured the amount of Amazonian rain forest cut down by intrepid entrepreneurs in the search for the willing investor, it would match the number of quarter pounders consumed by a population the size of Wales every week.

In short, the pitch consumes the entrepreneur's energy, intellect and emotional reserves in ways which can lead to flatulence, obesity and short sighted, short term gratification.

They may be terrific at hooking investors into the short term buy in and medium term buy out: but whether they contribute to a region's long term economic health is another matter altogether.

If in doubt, say 'Creative'.

You're in a meeting; it's bumbling along; minutes are handed out and people frown and glare or pass out in the heat of the moment. There's mutterings under breaths; there's sighs, grunts and the occasional fart.

Some bright spark says *'what we need is a creative something something something'* and suddenly the whole room has lit up in technicolour: the sighs become shouts, the grunts become groans of delight and the farts metamorphose into sounds of rejoicing: the whoopee cushion is something we all want to sit on now the creativity cat is out of the bag.

Because make no mistake: dropping the 'c' word into any business venture is bound to galvanise your workforce, impress your investors and stoke up the heat of admiration upon you. It doesn't matter what the *something something something* is (you could have equally said *blahdy blahdy blah):* the fact that you've introduced the 'c' word to your proposal is what's fired up the meeting.

In the olden days we would have used the words *'magic'* and the effect would have been the same. These days, *'creativity'* has replaced the word for *'magic'* (and *'alchemy'* and *'smoke and mirrors'* and *'snake oil'* for that matter) and the world and it's business offices have become far happier places as a result.

So, if in future you're stuck in a turgid negotiation, CRM update or monitoring moment, just drop the word *'creative'* into proceedings and see your business proposition grow wings and fly to the heavens.

It may not last long up there as it gets too close to the sun, but your colleagues and customers will thank you for liberating them from their non-magical daily grinds.

How to love your business plan: write it backwards.

Roger, Rachel and Rezillo all have one thing in common when it comes to their business plan: they hate it.

Or more accurately, they hate the act of writing it. They've joined forces in Aberdeen in an attempt to break into the Scottish patisserie market and although they can't stop arguing about the merits of choux over flaky pastry and squirm when it comes to having to talk to each other about the best conditions for making Crème Anglaise, the one thing that does bind them is their mutual loathing of All Things Business Plan.

This is hardly surprising because at school, they, like so many talented entrepreneurs were completely useless when it came to dealing with the rigours of the national curriculum and the challenging stretch targets in literacy they were set when they were seven years old. Our 3 'R's of patisserie completely bottled it when it came to the 3 'R's of reading, riting and rithmetic.

The fact that those 3 'R's are meaningless and should be the 'RWA's is irrelevant and we'll let that pass for the moment.

The result of the 3 'R's literacy failure at an early age has meant that now it comes to the need to write some substantial business plan for future investors, they are at a complete loss.

They stare at blank sheets of paper, they download templates galore from the internet, try writing them out in their best handwriting but all to no avail: the damn plan won't get written.

So, the intrepid entrepreneur who is passionate about their business but filled with dread when it comes to writing about it has to go back to basics when it comes to getting that plan together and rediscover earlier moments in their lives when writing was still a pleasure and not the grind it became at school.

Here are some tips that helped them in that process.

1.   Write absolute rubbish. Enjoy writing rubbish. Don't worry about the order of that rubbish or whether it's spelt correctly or any other grammatical niceties. Just churn out as much garbage as you can with the thought of your business foremost in your mind. You can edit it
afterwards. The most important thing at the beginning is to generate. Anything.

2.   Write anywhere. If you prefer to write standing up, laying down, on the floor or on the walls, go ahead. Some of the best business plans started off as graffiti.

3.   Use any implement on any medium you like. Sticks in mud, felt tip pens on flip chart, blood in the sand. Don't obsess about sitting at your laptop and laboriously typing it out word by painful word. Someone else can always do that conventional job for you later.

4. Write it backwards. Too many business plan models insist you gaze into the future and predict all kinds of imponderables. Another way is to imagine you've just finished your first two years and you're looking back at what you achieved. Just describe in the past tense rather than fretting about what might or might not happen in an impossible future tense. The fact that you can place yourself up a mountain of hindsight and convey all that you've created means the plan is a record of achievement, not a hyperbolic statement of intent.

The 3 'R's of Scottish patisserie took to this approach with gusto and soon ended up with content which was rapidly converted into the tastiest business flan they'd ever concocted.

CHAPTER TWO: THE ENTREPRENEUR

Eight More Tips and Tricks for Business Start Ups

1. How to clone an Entrepreneur
2. Beware the Boot Camp
3. Your Heroic Journey
4. Switch off the Cop in Your Head
5. Your Entrepreneurial Prayer
6. The role of the Artist Entrepreneur
7. Stop Using the 'F' Word!
8. Entrepreneurs do not have Magic DNA

How to clone an Entrepreneur.

Many businesses are the result of the passion, vision and sheer bloody mindedness of an entrepreneur whose life's vision is completely dedicated to creating an enterprise which can solve a long standing problem to humanity and with any luck make some money for that entrepreneur in the meantime.

And when I say completely dedicated that's exactly what they have to be: from dawn to dusk, without deviation, hesitation or repetition as Nicholas Parsons used to remind the Just a Minute panel on their weekly half hour trip into the light fantastic of Radio 4 easy listening.

Without repetition though for many entrepreneurs is a difficult concept. As they begin their entrepreneurial journey they soon find that they have to be not only jack of all trades but master of them all too: whether this be their ability to create product, market it, sell it, fill in the tax returns and keep the bank happy, the budding entrepreneur is soon faced with a stark dilemma: how can they clone themselves in order to make sure their business vision can grow and meet the ever expanding demands that are being made of them?

Many entrepreneurs find novel solutions to the cloning dilemma. Some have experimented with stem cell technology, often with remarkable effect. Richard Branson for example has cloned himself many times over in order to run the diverse business empire he has established since opening that first Virgin record shop in Tottenham Court Road in 1972.

How else do you think he has been such a success in industries such as railways, insurance and pet food?

Others have taken more prosaic routes to cloning themselves: establishing a franchise for example is one simple yet expensive route to ensure that other people think, act and behave and in exactly the same way you do.

A more risky approach is to write a job description, employ someone, give them a training manual and trust in their ability to absorb everything you wrote, everything you think you wrote and everything you should have wrote and then act in a manner which would indicate that you have completed an effective mind meld, in the best Star Trek tradition.

The trouble with expecting a mind meld to solve the cloning dilemma is that human beings tend to demonstrate the annoying tendency of individualism. This is an anathema to the entrepreneur as the only individuality they are concerned about is their own: it is, after all, their vision, passion and sheer bloody mindedness which has led to the need for cloning themselves in the first place.

The challenge for the entrepreneur is not so much about how they clone themselves, but how they welcome difference and diversity and can tolerate behaviours which might not fit easily in their driven psyches.

If the entrepreneur can embrace the concept that they cannot be everything to everyone all of the time, then they stand a much better chance of letting others embrace their vision rather than it becoming everyone else's nightmare.

Beware the Boot Camp!

Intense learning in any context, and particularly the business start up community, is often referred to as a Boot Camp. It's an entertaining metaphor as it conjures up images of drill sergeants shouting instructions into the faces of some hapless recruit who has to stand stock still whilst receiving a volley of verbal abuse, all in the name of building character and mental resilience.

We hear frequent anecdotes about initiation rites which involve subjecting said hapless recruit to various degrading and dehumanising activities, none of which will be repeated here for the fear of encouraging you to throw up in public. No doubt you can use your own imagination when it comes to combining images of bodily fluids, kitchen utensils and small furry animals.

Boot camps are frequently correctional too: taking to its bosom cohorts of wayward youth, correctional boot camps are focused on righting behavioural wrongs and leaving the recipients under no delusion that if they continue in their erroneous ways, their guts will be traded in for garters and there'll be no discounts for multiple offending and mass apologies.

The boot camp is a seductive metaphor in business start up circles given its promise of rapid growth, profit generation and economic impact which is irreversible, sticky and worth the pain that's inflicted on its happy campers. But there's a major problem with the metaphor which is not just about whether entrepreneurs should subject themselves to volleys of abuse and cattle prods to steer them towards their economic nirvana.

The problem at the heart of all boot camps – the military, correctional and business – is their emphasis on increasing procedural knowledge (i.e. skill acquisition) at the expense of increasing their propositional knowledge (I.e. subject knowledge) and building their personal knowledge.

The boot camp regime doesn't concern itself with why you should learn new skills, just that you should. It doesn't equip campers with the ability to ask questions about those skills or to consider the power of their own knowledge. Neither is it the slightest bit interested in asking whether the skills it values are appropriate. Its sole mantra is skills, skills and more skills, coupled in many cases to a zeal for testing personalities to destruction.

Now this is fine up to a point: no-one is going to seriously dispute the value of learning skills when it comes to improving your life or business chances. If you can't read or write for example you might as well be living in a foreign country for all the sense you will be able to make of your environment.

But skills alone are not enough. You might be a perfectly competent sales person when it comes to performing a sales script over the phone but when it comes to understanding how the market is formed and how it operates, how your product might be modified to generate a stronger emotional connection with your customer, how your behaviours influence others and what other people have learnt from similar challenges in similar contexts, then as an entrepreneur you need access to other types of knowledge, namely your personal knowledge and propositional knowledge of the field you operate in.

Without access to those knowledges, your skill base, your procedural knowledge – is likely to condemn you to repetitive behaviours which may rapidly become obsolete.
Without those other types of knowledge, your skills turn you into a performing dog: entertaining in the short term but ultimately useless when the world decides it has no need for performing dogs any longer, which, given the rate of change of the global economy is likely to happen sooner rather than later.

So, a skills driven bootcamp for entrepreneurs is misguided in many ways: as a metaphor it's inappropriately aggressive; as a model of learning for entrepreneurs who need to develop their full learning complement of knowledge types and wisdom within a rounded personality it's painfully lacking.

So what might be a suitable alternative? What might be a more powerful metaphor to gather motivated entrepreneurs who have expressed a desire to improve but who may be suspicious of places which traditionally impart propositional knowledge and on a good day, enhance their personal knowledge? The Greenhouse? The Bakery? The Holiday Camp?

All come with their own fair share of metaphorical limitations. As Alfred Korzybski once said, the map is not the territory.

Starting from the basis that a developmental programme needs to embrace all three kinds of knowledge – personal, propositional and procedural – if it's going to improve the effectiveness of the entrepreneur is at least a step in the right direction away from the wilderness of the boot camp and towards something richer, more complex and ultimately more economically effective.

Your Heroic Journey.

It's tough out there in start up land in lots of different ways and it's not until you start out on that start up road that you realise how tough it is. Whether this be starting up a business, or starting up a new chapter in your life, the heroic journey you are about to embark upon is never clear until you're in the middle of it.

You have an idea, a dream, a vision but you're stuck in a day job you don't quite know how you got into and even less of an idea of how to get out of. Your dream becomes an itch, your itch becomes a preoccupation, your preoccupation becomes obsessive and there comes a point where you just have to shake that obsessing monkey off your back, get out of the house and get on with it.

But you have a personal finance history which resembles Krakatoa with cash leaking out in every direction, creditors chasing you for debts you incurred many moons ago when the world was your oyster and the friendly face of your bank manager was offering you unlimited friendly credit at friendly rates of interest with nothing in the way of security other than to demonstrate that you had a friendly piggy bank hidden under your bed.

But those days are long gone and the friendly faces have gotten greyer, bleaker and less friendly. The piggy bank is still under the bed and it has the grand total of £17.14p in mixed copper denominations weighing it down. Much like you feel when you wake up in the morning.

You want to make something happen from this business idea but quickly realise that in order to do that you need other people on board; people like employees or apprentices but you soon realise that they don't have anything like the same degree of vested interest in your obsession as you do and would be much rather counting the hours down till they can down tools and head off to the nearest bar along with their apprentice mates who care even less about the businesses they have been entrusted with.

You look at the concept of zero hours contracts and wonder who in their right mind would sign a contract that guarantees them nothing in exchange for their personal liberty and you realise at this point that growing your business with new staff is not all it's cracked up to be.

You want so much to make your latent vision manifest and engage the help of any number of advisors, supporters, coaches, mentors and agencies who all come to with shiny happy faces whilst waving bundles of forms at you. This is promising until they tell you that you've used up your 12 hours allowance of support and now can no longer be of assistance, thank you very much it's been great working with you and goodbye and by the way what's your post code?

Your family are screaming at you to stay in your job, your advisors are screaming at you to get out of your job, your bootcamp director screams at you end of and everyone everywhere is screaming their own agendas through the megaphone that your business has become to them. *"Grow grow grow! Sell sell sell! Jobs jobs jobs!"*

And all you want to do is make a difference, however big, however small, just make a difference to the part of the planet you currently occupy.

There are promises everywhere: of expense accounts, of tax breaks, of foreign jaunts, of funding, of assistance, of GVA, of debt, of equity, of lives lost, gained and squandered: everyone everywhere is promising you the moon or at least pointing up to the sky and screaming *'There it is! Now go get it!'* They may as well add *'Fido'* for all the use their exhortations are.

So yes, it's tough out there in start up land in lots of different ways and it's not until you start out on that start up road that you realise how tough it is. But at the end of the road, the joy about the heroic journey you are part of is that you can look at yourself in the mirror in the morning and say to yourself: *"I did that. I took those risks, I made it happen, I made that difference."* The business start up heroic journey doesn't get much better than that.

Switch off the Cop in Your Head.

Many tentative entrepreneurs when faced with the prospect of writing about their business – whether it be their business plan, their marketing strategy or a Dear John letter that's shaping up for their relationship that's gone sour due to their emotional over investment in their business – frequently get stuck after the first line about what to say in the second line of their entrepreneurial confession.

Maggie was faced with her own literary challenge when it came to presenting her unique approach to improving the world by setting up a time bank business.

She worried about the syntax, she fretted about the grammar, the spelling and all those other 1001 secretarial niceties which guaranteed her prose drained the blood out of her dream and left her venture laying dead on the slab of the business plan page.

Her previous educational experiences of writing in school was partly to blame for the Cop in her Head which pointed out everything that was wrong about her writing as she tried committing it to the page.

"You can't say this, you can't say that; you mustn't over-claim, you mustn't undersell; you don't use that word like that, that colon never goes there..."

The Cop in Maggie's Head worked overtime directing her writing energies like a deranged traffic cop in the middle of the Champs Élysées. All she needed was a peaked hat, a whistle and six pairs of arms waving frantically at her business plan and the picture would have been complete.

The trouble with the Cop in Maggie's Head is was that it insisted on her writing correctly rather than writing with her own voice. To counteract this, she tried writing rubbish, writing it quickly and writing without judging the quality or sense of what she was able to spew forth on to the page. Above everything, she had to write it out – warts and all.

And spew she did. Before long she had pages and pages of garbage: half formed sentences, odd words, noisy punctuation – the works. She wrote backwards, from right to left, sitting down and standing up, with large green felt tip markers and thin black biros.

She wrote whilst she sang, whilst she walked, she wrote on paper and on the walls; she used flip chart, old newspapers and A4: above all she quietened the Cop In Her Head and after 30 minutes of manic scribbling was able to sit back, read and marvel at some of the surprises she had generated for herself.

Once she had given voice to everything in her head about the business, she was able to sift through it, edit and shape it and polish it to her heart's content. Not only had she produced the first draft of her business plan and the framework of her marketing strategy, her Dear John letter took on added vitality and she was able to disentangle herself from the Cop in Her Life who had been trying to block her every business aspiration since the morning she woke up and realised her what her life's mission needed to be.

So, whatever you do with your business plan: just make sure you write rubbish, you write it fast, and you write it out. Switch off the Cop in Your Head and you may just switch off the Cop in Your Life.

Your Entrepreneurial Prayer.

To the great shadowy entrepreneurial
spark in the sky (or wherever offers
free office space and fibre optic broadband):

Allow me, enable me, permit me,
Challenge me, drive me, ignore me.
Pet me, fret me, set me up to fail me,
And let me get right back up again.

The role of the artist entrepreneur.

Maybe, just maybe the artist entrepreneur could answer the questions of:

How are we going to manage when public sector funding has dried up?
When audiences are becoming more conservative?
When the corporates are opting for the safe and secure?
When the clichés are running rings around new thinking opportunities?

Maybe, just maybe the artistic entrepreneur can see opportunities for new productions and new services?

Maybe, just maybe the artist entrepreneur can carve out new marketplaces rather than be beholden to preconceived ideas of what constitutes the marketplace?

Maybe, just maybe the artist entrepreneur could ignore boundaries of professional, amateur and community and facilitate engagement processes which work with the power of the artistic vision rather than the pragmatism of the cultural realpolitik?

Maybe, just maybe the artist entrepreneur could reimagine a future which is based on vision, critical engagement and personal and social transformation?

Maybe, just maybe the artist entrepreneur could galvanise the artist to wake up to what their power and possibilities are, and to quell their worries and anxieties?

Stop using the 'F' word!

Many proto-businesses in their initial start up phase get carried away with the idea that there is a golden stash of cash out there, called funding, which will help them in all their endeavours to get their business up and running.

Funding is a panacea to all start up ills they argue: without it, there is no business; without it, they have no livelihood; without it, they are unable to turn their unique, gleaming shiny idea into a world beater which will eventually see them rubbing shoulders with the likes of Richard Branson, Terry Leahy and Mary Portas.

Trouble is, Funding – the F word – is a like a huge magnet, distorting what the proto business is likely to achieve, distorting its owners expectations and exaggerating the sunny vistas ahead.

What many proto businesses don't get is that their great idea is not necessarily a great business: not because it can't attract funding, but because at the heart of it, it is highly unlikely to generate income on its own terms.

A great idea needs eventually to be involved in the messy business of trade. Someone somewhere needs to want your great idea and is prepared to trade you something in exchange for it.

Usually that trade, for better or worse, involves the transfer of cash from one person to another in an act of buying and selling. This generates income for the business which is used for the business's future livelihood. It is not the same as funding and should never be confused with funding.

Entrepreneurs do not have magic DNA.

Hilary is anxious that she doesn't think she has the same drive or entrepreneurial qualities that Hilary Devey on the Dragons Den demonstrates. She thinks her transport business is going to flounder as a result.

Richard, an earlier start up, was similarly depressed that he doesn't have the same burning ambition as Richard Branson and that his blooming internet flowershop website will wither and die accordingly.

What Hilary and Richard are finding difficult to accept is that their entrepreneurial abilities are not merely described by their own psychological profiles, but are as dependent on their family and social contexts as they are on their own IQs, personal action plans and own brand of cussidness and obstinacy.

Contrary to much popular opinion, the success of the entrepreneur or thrusting young business person does not depend on them having bucket loads of magical DNA in their gene pool.

Whatever the Richards or the Hilarys of the world might tell you, or what the press might suggest about them, their success is due as much as it is to being in the right place in the right family and social context as it is their own personal and psychological make up.

Young Hilarys and Richards alike could do their business ideas a power of good if they could literally start at home when they start their planning: see who is around them, who can help them, what they can offer in return and progress knowing that their success will be down to the gravitational pull of their relationships with their friends and their families: not their personal charisma or ability to exploit budding musicians who will go on to change the world of popular music

CHAPTER THREE: DOING IT

Eight More Tips and Tricks for Business Start Ups

1. Start your own National Day
2. Why you need more sorcerers than apprentices
3. Don't kiss what you can kick
4. How to work in, on
and under your business
5. Starting a business is like living in Second Life
6. Build it and they will come (or not)
7. Growing your business with The Spice Girls
8. Yes, You May

Start your own National Day of (insert business sector here).

It's National Porridge Day!

And yet another national day of something promoting something that's never needed promoting in the past. Spinach, verrucas and now porridge. As everyone in the Britain's Got Talent generation knows, everyone and everything has a right for the national spotlight and today it's the turn of porridge and its variants.

So, well done porridge for making it this far. In an age of Pot Noodle, Alcopops and instant show biz gratification your staying power is astonishing. Perhaps we could all take a leaf out of your cooking book and sustain ourselves for longer, further and faster. You truly are the Olympian of cereals.

So, if you're looking to push your product or service out of its promotional comfort zone and up to its limits of plausibility, why not start a National Day of your very own?

Whether it's pizza toppings, pet insurance or vajazzles, no-one will contradict you and your business may hit the terrifying trending heights of Twitter in less time than it takes to cook a bowl of Scott's Porridge Oats.

Damn it. I've succumbed to the hype. Well done porridge people, you've done it again.

Why you need more sorcerers than apprentices.

When we're made redundant, we might initially welcome the opportunity to loosen the shackles of an old job; only to find later that we've taken those very same shackles into the new job.

Brian has worked for years in Leeds in an established catering suppliers which like everything else these days faces some serious challenges to its existence. Unfortunately for Brian that means it now has to let him go.

Brian semi-jokes about not wanting to be let go and that he's very happy to stay hidden amongst the pots and pans, but he knows his protestations are in vain: *'being let go of'* euphemistically hides the fact that he's being made redundant.

So, with his pay off, a substantial customer database and potentially six months of development time in his backpack, Brian has set up a new kitchen suppliers doing pretty much the same thing as he was doing in his old one – albeit in a leaner and meaner fashion with an emphasise on technology for paleo-catering.

His natural instinct has been to set about looking for staff who he can build the business with. He's worked up job descriptions, person specifications and all the usual paraphernalia of what it takes to engage other people in your business.

But this rush to growth means he has missed an opportunity to rethink how he could really get to grips with how the business engages people over and beyond providing rabbit skinning technology to customers on time and to budget.

Brian assumes that employing staff will automatically grow the business when in fact it probably won't. Employment can generate many different senses of entitlement for people: they do a job and they get paid for it; they work a certain number of hours, take a certain number of days leave, can reasonably expect sick pay and all the other benefits that a mature workforce in a mature employer can reasonably expect to enjoy.

The problem is that a new start up is not a mature business and not necessarily a reasonable place to work.

It is fragile, uncertain of its place in the world and whether it is likely to survive out in the wilds of the market place beyond the first year is open to a lot of doubt.

There's a forest load of wild animals, poison ivy and bear traps to face if you're setting up a new business and the last thing you want is a co-pioneer complaining about their employment contract.

A new start doesn't need solutions imported to it from mature businesses with notions such as 'employing staff' driving its thinking. It needs new solutions which confront the needs of its newness.

The new start up doesn't need staff at all – people who will honour contracts and deliver a job to the best of their ability in return for a negotiated remuneration – but generators: people who not only deliver the business core activity but who can also generate more activity, more income and emulate the entrepreneur who has brought them to the party.

What Brian really needs are people who can generate something from nothing, to make value from where there was none before, to act as alchemists rather than as commi-chefs who can follow recipes to the letter but who don't have the inspirational touch which invents, creates and conjures further opportunities from thin air.

Unless he can find those energies, Brian is likely to find that his new business will be letting him go in much the same way as the old one did.

He needs to engage a lot more sorcerers – not more apprentices - in his new kitchens of the paleo-north.

Don't kiss what you can kick.

Some start ups emerge from the public sector, some from the dole and many more these days, given the parlous state of British manufacturing, from the private sector.

Agnes is one such start up who wants to take hold of the Cupcake market in Leicester by the scruff of the neck and make it squeal till it recognises there is only one way of making and selling cupcakes: her way.

Whilst she has rapidly grown the business due to the marketplace's infatuation with all things cupcake and employed several new staff, she has imported the staff development culture from her previous private sector employer when it comes to working with them: *"Don't kiss what you can kick"*.

Her new staff have provided her with a whole range of arses to kick, whip or boot into shape which she does with enthusiasm. She's already installed a CCTV camera in the office toilet allegedly to check on staffs comfort break habits but more than likely to check on the state of their arses.

She is convinced the only good staff arse is one bent over the production line, adhering to production targets and keeping their other orifice – their mouth – well and truly shut.

Now, Agnes' approach may well have worked wonders in the likes of British Leyland, the British Mining industry, the British Steel industry and the rest of the UK's successful manufacturing past.

But unhappily for her, it won't work in the disrespectful world of the start up.

New staff don't want to be viewed as arses. They want to be involved in the business action and to buy into her methods through encouragement, excitement and a sense of thrill – not the chill that comes with being viewed as a rear end commodity which has two potential states of being kicked or kissed.

Employing new staff in a new start is potentially the best and worst of all possible worlds. It's the thrill of the first date, of selling the new product or service, of sharing the promise as well as the load: but equally the fear of not being quite good enough, of not meeting the others needs and of only providing a stop gap until something better comes along.

But in creating her business family, Agnes will soon have to stop regarding her family members as troublesome arses and more like prospective stakeholders in her long term future: because when the cupcake market implodes, she will need all the help she can get to ensure her business doesn't go down the pan with it.

How to work in, on and under your business.

Cathy wants to set up a small newspaper business; Dennis wants to build an online clothing emporium; Carmelita wants to sell imported beetle vapour.

Diverse they may be but there is one thing common to all these three start ups who met in a lift and immediately tried pitching their business to each other.

All three knew the stuff of their business – the content, the processes, the qualities of what they were developing. They'd all be working in their businesses for many years and were intimately connected to what it was their business consisted of.

All three had their business plans in various states of disrepair which reflected their partial knowledge of working on their business: the cash flow, the marketing, the SEOS.

But perhaps more importantly than working in and on their business, all three know deep down that what really really mattered was their understanding of what was going on under the business: the stuff which told them why their business was important to other people, why it mattered and what had led them to deciding to working in and on their fledgling business.

Cathy was driven by a desire to improve reading skills in very young people, something she'd missed out on when she was young; Dennis wanted to support emerging economies in Vietnam having been involved as a soldier in the war in the 1960s; and Carmelita was obsessed with the quest to find a cure for the lung cancer which had killed her mother's family for generations.

Working in the business is important; working on the business is essential; but working under the business will provide Cathy, Dennis and Carmelita with the energy and motivation to sustain their businesses through the long dark nights of recession and economic challenge.

Starting a business is like living in Second Life.

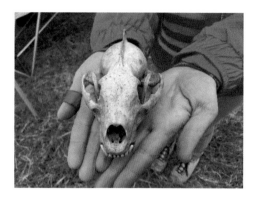

Jeremy has been successfully trading himself for many years. Rather than promoting a product which can change the world, his service is closer to home: it's his own identity. Jeremy is widely known for providing valuable skills in the field of home tutoring.

He's travelled near and far, coaching and mentoring students from his home in Glasgow and across Scotland and has generated a useful income which helps him sustain his collection of birds of prey.

The challenge that Jeremy has faced as a sole trader is something that faces all of us: Anno Domini. He's getting older by the day (like all of us) and as the years go by, he's facing competition from younger tutors who are able to enthuse and entertain in a way that is proving irresistible to Jeremy's clients.

In years gone by, tutors were valued for their ability to do just that: tute. This may had involved coaching, mentoring, guiding and some advice giving, but fundamentally the success of their work was defined by how good a tute they could give.

These days, in common with the expectation that full time teachers face, tutoring is no longer enough. These days, tutors also have to be project managers, entertainers, performers, odd job facilitators, welfare managers, credit specialists and mind readers. To tute is no longer enough.

Jeremy is waking up daily to the uneasy realisation that not only is his skill set out of date, but that his customers are looking at him and saying to themselves, *"He's great Jeremy but…"* And there they will add any phrase which points to their belief that Jeremy is too old to carry out the work any longer.

Ageism in any walk of life is an appalling way of relating to people; but when customers steer clear of your services because of their perception about the implications of the older work force, this is particularly hard.

This is a key moment when sole traders need to trade up and reinvent themselves as a business. The creation of a new business identity which can put out in the market place is an ideal way of countering customers covert ageism.

A new business identity will allow Jeremy to reinvent himself and his economic activity by presenting his activities to customers in a way which emphasises his youthful energy whilst simultaneously being able to draw on the maturity of his experience.

Setting up a business if you're a sole trader is a bit like joining Second Life with an avatar you have created. It allows you to present yourself as you want and can confound people's stereotypes and expectations. It can allow you to reform and perform your identity in many new ways, as well as providing an umbrella for future collaborators to join you under.

Jeremy has jumped into the equivalent of second Life with a vengeance this week and is promoting his tutoring skills in all their glory and diversity through his identity of the Golden Eagle. His customer base has jumped up almost overnight.

The fact he is 86 is neither here nor there; Jeremy's second life identity has knocked any number of years off his customers perceptions and he's out there again, trading, touring and tuting.

His birds of prey can rest easy in the aviary. They've been spared a future back in the wild for a few more years to come.

Build it and they will come (or not).

Fitzcarraldo was the Werner Herzog film about the entrepreneur Brian Sweeney Fitzgerald who decided to build an opera house in the Amazon Jungle by pulling a small boat over a mountain enlisting the help of several thousand Amazonian Indians many of whom died in this doomed venture.

Herzog's film itself was hardly a smooth business proposition what with lead actor Klaus Kinski threatening to walk out and Herzog himself retaliating by offering to kill Kinski if he as much took a foot outside the troubled film camp.

But Fitzcarraldo – the entrepreneur of entrepreneurs – had, for all his cussed waywardness, an awesome business vision for his opera house: *'build it and they will come'*.

However no one ever seems to have caught sight of our hero's business plan – he certainly doesn't refer to it any dialogue that Kinski utters – and the question of who 'they' are is never quite clear. Western European opera buffs? Brazilians in search of rarified European culture? Crocodiles in search of food supplied by the tourists who have fallen foul of the myriad of bugs viruses and small goat size anemones which cover the Amazonian forest floor?

We are not sure and neither was Fitzcarraldo – and more likely than not, he didn't really care who they were, as long as they came.

Unhappily for many of us lesser entrepreneurs, *'build it and they will come'* is as tantalising a proposition for us as it was for Fitz. It has generated its own trails of failed business plans, mad cap ventures, impossible business scenarios and hair brained schemes which look great on paper, even better in film but utterly doomed in the nasty jungle floor of business reality.

'Build it and they will come' is a great motivational force – but it needs to be coupled with an equal and opposite force which says:

"and what do they get out of coming along to your magnificent edifice? And how are you going to get them to come along, especially if your proposal is set in the urban equivalent of the Amazon? And who is they in the first place? Your mum and dad? Nearest and dearest? Complete strangers who don't know – yet – that their life's mission will not be completed until they have visited your own personal opera house?"

Build it and they will come has provided some great business stories in recent times – but if you want to avoid the substantial collateral damage of dead bodies on and off set and the spectre of white elephants littering your neighbourhood, then be clear on the who, the what, the where, the how, the when and the why of the 'they'.

Growing your business with The Spice Girls.

Carla runs a very successful sandwich shop in Luton and has made a tidy little business dealing in all kinds of meat, vegetable and bread combinations: baps, buns, wraps and baguettes, there's nothing Carla doesn't know about how to surround animal protein with bread of any of its multiple variants.

She's doing so well that she's been thinking about growing her business and she's taken some advice from the local business development agency who have been very helpful in helping her understand the pressure that growing her business will have on her cash flow, supplier demands and customer satisfaction.

But they've not addressed the fundamental issue about business growth. In asking her 'Do you want to grow your business?' and then providing her with all sorts of useful information about how to grow it, they've not recognised that the most important verb in that question is not 'to grow'.

The most important verb in that question is the 'W' word, the word about wanting, about desiring, about hungering after, about feeling something so strongly that no obstacle will get in your way, that no hurdle will block you from your intention and no stone will be left unturned to get You what You Want: which in Carla's case is a sandwich making emporium.

"I'll tell you what I want, what I really really want" was, we are told, the rallying cry of both Constantin Stanislavski, the well known Russian teacher who knew a bit about training actors, and the 1990s phenomenon that was the Spice Girls.

With their emphasis on desire, both Stanislavski and the Spice Girls knew a thing or two about the training of entrepreneurs and how they could apply their intentions and desires to growing their businesses.

The thing is however, in order to grow your business, you have to do things differently. It's all very well making sandwiches to your hearts content but to grow her business, to really really want to grow her business, Carla is going to have to step out from the loaves and bread cutters and pots of potted shrimp and hand those items over to someone else so that she can concentrate on getting the bigger job done: that of satisfying her desire to grow her business.

Her desire for growth is essential because without it she'll stay nested in the pots of potted shrimp, spreading low fat tastes-nothing-like butter spread all day, only to watch her competitor's desires take to the stage and slowly sideline Carla out of her beloved business.

This may be fine of course if all she wants to do is sell sandwiches – but growing her business will make different demands on her and she would be wise to think hard about what she wants, what she really really wants.

Yes, You May.

Sharon is in the throes of starting up her new business idea of selling coals to Newcastle. On one level it looks a fairly dubious proposition; the coal industry in Newcastle is heaving (or so we are led to believe); the last thing Newcastle needs is any more aspiring coal importers and in any case the railways aren't what they were so trying to get the black stuff into the city is more difficult than ever before.

However, Sharon is blessed with a supply of high grade magical coal which does what no other coal has ever done before; she has access to the key Tyneside decision makers and she can guarantee that her first import will put a smile on her bank managers face (well, assuming those faceless automatons have faces any longer).

What Sharon is struggling with is permission. She's looking for permission to set up the business and looking for an outside agency to say *"Yes, you may."* as opposed to the more ambivalent, *"Yes, you can"*.

"Can I really book that freight car?"
"Yes, you may."
"Can I really contract a volunteer to work with me? Is that legal?'
"Yes it is and yes you may."
"Can I really put my own logo on our website?"
"Yes you may, and yes you should and yes yes yes."

Such is the conversation. Many business start ups, like students in their final year at uni; or kids at the edge of the swimming pool who are about to make their first dive into the deep end; or anyone who is about to make the biggest decision of their life; are looking for just one thing: permission. For some-one to say:

"Yes. It's not illegal.
Yes. It's a good idea.
Yes. It will be hard work.
Yes. You might sink but on the other hand you might just swim.
Yes. Your coals are just the sort of coals people in Newcastle are looking for. Do it. And do it now."
"May I? Really?"
"Yes, you may."

Let Go

It's worth reminding the entrepreneur about the parents of his or her favoured business idea.

For all the glorification of the entrepreneur and their ideas, the reality is that those ideas have not come out of nowhere – they're the result of creative intercourse between various forces in the entrepreneur's life – whether this be their current boss, ex-partner or irritant down at the old Bull and Bush.

The entrepreneurs pet idea is the offspring of those intercourses and it's worth spending some thinking about the background of the idea's parents. Are they loaded? Royaled? Troubled? Are they likely to lead to some hybrid vigour in their offspring? Or are they so inbred that the idea is only ever likely to survive in a state of permanent hospitalisation, connected to the life support systems of funding, business support services and royal privilege?

For one thing is clear about the creative intercourse which leads to the business idea: it needs to have been generated by forces which need to be different, confident and vital: energies which will enable the business idea to stand on its own two shaky feet some time soon.

The entrepreneur is but a channel for those energies, and to misquote Khalil Gibran:

Your business is not your business.
It is the son and daughter of Life's longing for itself.
It comes through you but not from you,
And though it is with you yet it belongs not to you.
You may give it your love but not your thoughts,
For it has its own thoughts.
You may house its body but not its soul,
For its soul dwell in the house of tomorrow,
which you cannot visit, not even in your dreams.

You may strive to be like it,
but seek not to make it like you.
For life goes not backward nor tarries with yesterday.
You may give it your love but not your thoughts,
For it has its own thoughts.
You may house its body but not its soul,
For its soul dwells in the house of tomorrow,
which you cannot visit, not even in your dreams.

You are the bows from which your business
as living arrow is sent forth.
The archer sees the mark upon the path of the infinite,

and He bends you with His might
that His arrows may go swift and far.
Let your bending in the archer's hand be for
gladness;
For even as He loves the arrow that flies,
so He loves also the bow that is stable.

About the Author •

Awarded an MBE for services to arts based businesses in 2012, Nick is passionate about generating culturally inspiring and socially engaging creative businesses both nationally and internationally.

He has worked in all learning contexts from Early Years to Higher Education and Life Long Learning as teacher, tutor and curriculum leader or senior manager. He was awarded a unique scholarship for a PhD in Creativity and Learning from Creative Partnerships which he completed at the University of Hull in 2008 and was then awarded Honorary Fellowships in Education at both the University of Hull and University of Tasmania in Australia.

In recent years he has been especially focused on designing and delivering a range of business start up programmes within the creative and cultural sectors across the UK. For him, the essence of start up is about regeneration: of the individual, their community and the wider society in which they operate.

It's is about re-visioning a new future and constructing a new world which is better than the one which was there before. It's about fusing creative practice, learning and enterprise through meaningful and purposeful activity which not only satisfies the financial bottom line but aspires to generate the top lines of cultural and social impact too.

Whilst he has worked in the public, private and social enterprise sectors across the UK, he has been especially inspired by the international collaborations he has participated in with partners in Australia, Barbados, Bulgaria, Denmark, Germany, India, Lithuania, Italy, FYR Macedonia, Nigeria, Norway, Oman, Portugal, Serbia, South Africa and Trinidad and St. Lucia.

He says:

"We may have all come from vastly different backgrounds but one thing has bound us all: the interplay of culture, education and enterprise which is at the heart of personal and social regeneration."

Contact Details

Nick Owen Publishing
Nottingham
UK

richardnyowen@msn.com
www.nicko.com
@DrNickOMBE

23698232R00048

Printed in Great Britain
by Amazon